Library of Congress Cataloging in Publication Data

Young, Miriam
  If I drove a tractor.

  SUMMARY: A young boy imagines himself driving a variety of tractors.
  1. Tractors—Juvenile literature. [1. Tractors] I. Quackenbush, Robert, illus.
TL233.3.Y68   72-5142
ISBN 0-688-40041-8
ISBN 0-688-50041-2 (lib. bdg.)

MIRIAM YOUNG

IF I DROVE A TRACTOR

ILLUSTRATED BY ROBERT QUACKENBUSH

LOTHROP, LEE & SHEPARD CO./ NEW YORK

I'm going to drive a tractor
When I grow up
I mean
Some kind of motored wrecking
Or building machine.

If I had a farm tractor, I'd plow the empty lot next to our apartment house. I'd sit between the big wheels, churning up the ground three furrows at a time. Then I'd get my seed-drill tractor and plant the whole thing with corn. And late in summer, when the corn was ready, I'd invite my friends Ernest and Linda and the other kids to a corn roast. They'd all agree it was better to have a cornfield there than another parking lot.

Or maybe it would be good to have a back-hoe and dig a swimming pool there. I'd hop in the rear seat facing backwards, and start the digger going. With its stabilizers spread like legs, its digging arm stretched up like a neck and the digger sticking out like a head, the back-hoe would look like some pre-historic monster chewing up the ground. And I'd be a fearless rider, sitting on its back.

But a swimming pool wouldn't be big enough for all my friends, so maybe I'd better have a bulldozer. Then I could make a pond where the junk yard is. I'd sit in the cab with the caterpillar treads jerking along, pushing away old tires and rusted bedsprings and other junk. BRMM-CRASH ! I'd tear into everything. "Watch out!" I'd call to stray cats. "Don't get hurt." I'd wait while a mother cat took her kittens away. Then—BOOM-CRASH ! I'd bulldoze everything in my path and leave the place ready for a pond.

If I found a shelf of rock when I was digging, I'd make holes in it with an air drill—*Drrrttt Drrrttt*. I'd fill them with dynamite, push the plunger of my compressor and WHAM! the rock would explode. Then I'd get my power shovel to scoop up the pieces. I'd pull a lever, and the bucket would bite into the stones, spilling a few from its jaws like an animal with its mouth too full. I'd move the arm over a truck bed and the stone would come thundering down like an avalanche. And people on their way to work would stop to watch.

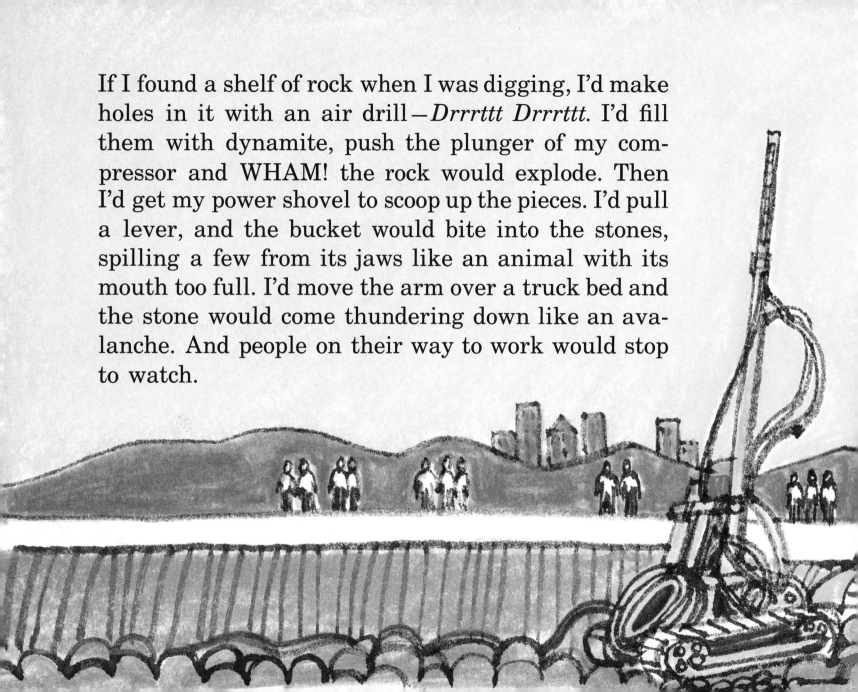

I'd have to take the stone someplace, so I'd build a new road to Grandma's house. But first I'd have to have a stone crusher to grind the stone to small pieces. *Crush, crash, gri-i-ind.* "Sorry about the noise," I'd say to Mother, "but won't it be nice to have a short cut?" I'd spread the stone on the roadbed with my monster grader. Then I'd get in my giant, ten-ton two-wheel roller and smooth it all down. And when the road was finished, we'd zip over to Grandma's in no time.

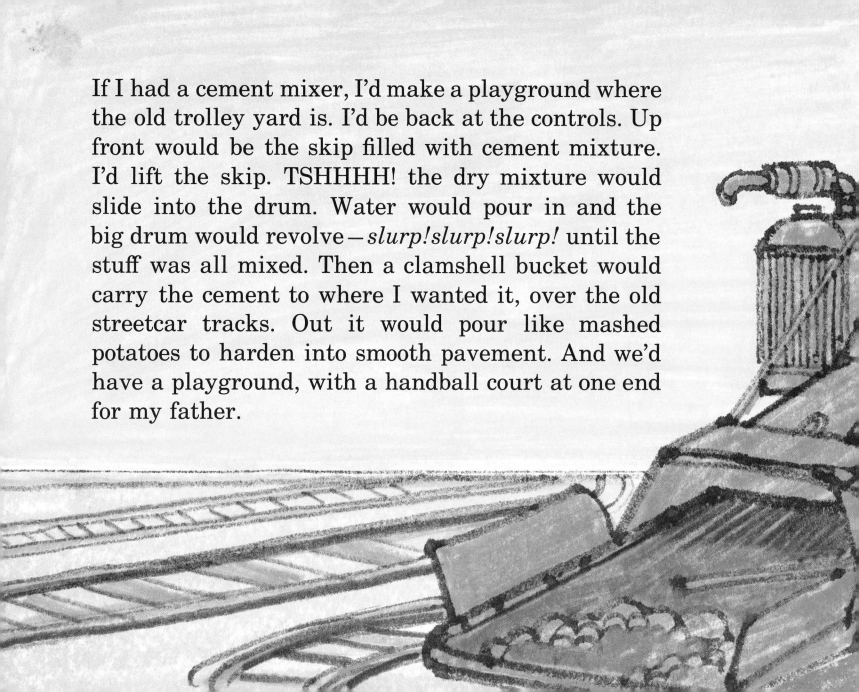

If I had a cement mixer, I'd make a playground where the old trolley yard is. I'd be back at the controls. Up front would be the skip filled with cement mixture. I'd lift the skip. TSHHHH! the dry mixture would slide into the drum. Water would pour in and the big drum would revolve—*slurp!slurp!slurp!* until the stuff was all mixed. Then a clamshell bucket would carry the cement to where I wanted it, over the old streetcar tracks. Out it would pour like mashed potatoes to harden into smooth pavement. And we'd have a playground, with a handball court at one end for my father.

Another machine I'd like to drive is the trencher. My trencher and I would lumber along the roadside where a trench was needed. I'd start the chains winding, *clank, clank, clank.* The buckets would go rattling around like cars on a Ferris wheel. Down, up and over, the sharp teeth would bite into the dirt— CR-UNCH! bringing it up and dumping it aside. Just like a sand toy I used to have, only big and real.

If I had a pile driver, I could sink piling for men who wanted to build a bridge over a swamp. I'd bring my machine to the edge of the swamp and hoist a pile. I'd put it in place in the swampy water and then BAM! drop my ram to drive it in. Then another pile — BAM! and another till the job was done. "There you are," I'd tell the men. "You can build your bridge now."

If somebody wanted an old warehouse knocked down, I'd be glad to do it if I had a wrecker. I'd get my wrecking machine in place, raise the "skull cracker" and send it swinging. CRASH! It would SLAM into the building. And SMASH! the old bricks would come down in a cloud of red dust. "Thanks a lot," they'd tell me when the job was done. "Not at all," I'd answer. "Call me any time."

Sometimes when men put up power lines, there's a tree in the way. If I had a mobile crane I'd say, "Don't cut down that tree—it's pretty. Let me cut the branches for you." I'd bring my crane over and climb to the platform. A control would send it up into the treetops. When it was high enough I'd get my power saw going—*Zrmmm! Zrmmm! Zrmmm!* and cut the branches that were in the way of the wires. Then I'd ride the platform down like a private elevator. And we'd all be glad to save the tree.

In summer when the grass grows high and weeds spring up, I'd like to drive a big tractor lawn mower in the park. I'd go humming along in the fresh evening air with my dog Perky beside me, the long cutter bars mowing a wide path. Drivers would wave as cars went by and people passing would take deep breaths of the scent of newly cut grass. "Such a nice, fresh smell!" they'd say, and smile as if to thank me, and Perky would bark, "You're welcome."

In the Fall it would be fun to drive the vacuum leaf-loader. I'd rumble along, moving the big hose over the fallen leaves like a giant vacuum cleaner. Ernest and Kenny and Linda would ride behind in a truck to do the raking, and Perky would ride in the cab with me. One day—just for fun—I'd put the vacuum into reverse and blow the leaves out instead of in. They'd fly around like colored snowflakes. We'd stamp on them to hear them crunch. Then I'd help to rake and gather them up again.

In winter when the snow is deep, I'd like to drive a big snow loader—the kind that has a melting machine inside. I'd grind along to where the snowplows had left big piles of snow against the curb and get my machinery going. *Scrape, crunch, grind,* I'd lift the big loads up and over into the back of the machine. BRBRMMM, it would start to melt. When the snow had turned to ice water, I'd pour it on the playground and make a skating rink. And we'd all go racing around.

So with tractors for digging and others to bulldoze,
Power shovels, steam rollers, mixers, back-hoes, Air
drills and graders and Diesel snow blowers, Trench-
ers and wreckers and powered lawn mowers . . .

If anyone wants me,
I'm sure to be found.
Driving some wonderful tractor around,
When I grow up.

1 2 3 4 5 77 76 75 74 73